All Families Are Different

ParentsCAN
3299 Claremont Way, Ste. 3
Napa, CA 94558

253.7444
www.parentscan.org

This book belongs to

_____

This book was given to me by

_____

All Families Are Different

Sol Gordon, Ph.D.

Illustrated by Vivien Cohen

 Prometheus Books

59 John Glenn Drive
Amherst, New York 14228-2119

Published 2000 by Prometheus Books

Inquiries should be addressed to
Prometheus Books, 59 John Glenn Drive, Amherst, New York 14228–2119.
VOICE: 716–691–0133, ext. 210.
FAX: 716–691–0137.
WWW.PROMETHEUSBOOKS.COM

11 10 09 08 07   9 8 7 6 5

Interior design by Grace M. Zilsberger

Library of Congress Cataloging-in-Publication Data

Gordon, Sol, 1923–
    All families are different / Sol Gordon : illustrated by Vivien Cohen.
        p.   cm.
    Summary: Discusses differences in families in today's society, and what makes each family special.
    ISBN 978-1-57392-765-9 (pbk. : alk. paper)
    1. Family—Juvenile literature. 2. Family—United States. I. Cohen, Vivien, ill.
II. Title.

99-52686
CIP

Printed in the United States of America on acid-free paper

This book is dedicated to

Marian Wright Edelman,
America's preeminent advocate for children.

Not long ago the word "family" meant children living with their own parents in the same place. They remained at home until they married. But, to tell the truth, this didn't always happen. People in those days had many problems. Lots of families were very poor. Most children didn't finish high school. They went to work and sometimes moved away from their families.

But things have changed. Now there are all kinds of families. Did you know that most girls and boys in America do not live with both of their parents? Only about four out of ten children live with their own mom and dad. There are other changes as well. Now almost all children finish high school and only when they are about eighteen years old do they start to work full-time or go to college.

Some kids are orphans—one or both of their parents have died. That's sad. But lots of these kids find good homes with caring adults and live with them as their children. And sometimes, children whose parents can't take care of them also grow up in new homes. In these new homes boys and girls are adopted, and their new parents love them as their own.

Sometimes kids can't stay with their moms and dads because their parents have big problems. The parents have to solve these problems before their children can return to be with them. These boys and girls live in what are called "foster homes," with adults who often have children of their own.

Here is a list of different types of families. Which one is most like yours? Maybe more than one of them tells what your family is like.

❑ Both parents leave home each day to be at their jobs.

❑ Mother or father takes care of the home and children while the other parent leaves the house to go to work.

❑ You live with one parent most of the time but you visit or live with the other parent sometimes.

Vivien Cohen

❏ You live with one parent, sometimes with your mother, who didn't marry your dad.

❏ You live with one parent and another one who is a stepparent. This means your mother or father chose a new partner who is not your parent.

❏ You live with a grandparent or maybe some other relative (an aunt, an uncle, or maybe a big brother or sister).

❏ You live with two parents of the same sex. It's like having two moms or two dads.

❏ You live in a foster home, where a family takes you into their house until you can go back to your own.

❏ You are the only child in the family or you have two or three or more brothers and sisters.

Did you find your family in this list? If you didn't then how is *your* family different?

So you can see there are many kinds of families. For some children, even though they might live with both parents, one parent, a stepparent, or some other relative, there may still be things about the family that are different from the families of their playmates and friends.

Some parents are of different races: the mother has white skin and the father's skin is black, or the father's skin is yellow and the mother's skin is brown. Two grown-ups with white skin, for example, may adopt a little boy or girl whose skin is brown, black, or yellow.

The way some parents worship is not always the same: the mom or dad may be a Catholic and the other is Jewish, or one is a Baptist and the other is a Hindu.

Lots of kids in America have parents and relatives who have moved here from countries all over the world. The mother's family may be from Greece and the father's from Mexico, or the father has German parents and the mother has relatives living in South America, or both parents were born in Mexico or Puerto Rico.

One family may have a big house and a swimming pool and the children have many toys and beautiful clothes, while another family lives in a simple house, has an old car that breaks down a lot, and sometimes there isn't enough money to buy everything the parents and children need or want.

There are families who have lived in the same house, on the same street, in the same town all their lives, and then there are other families who move a lot because of the mom's or dad's job.

There are people who make up all sorts of families in every neighborhood and town in America. Some parents don't speak English at all, and then there are others who can speak English and other languages. Some kids or parents can't walk or throw a ball. Other kids or parents may be in a wheelchair or are sick a lot. They may need a nurse or a helper to be with them and to help with getting dressed or with cooking a meal. Still other kids or parents might not be able to see or hear.

Some moms and dads have gone to college—they may be doctors, lawyers, dentists, accountants, computer programmers, or teachers—while other moms and dads work in stores in the mall, make the computers we use, or put cars together in a big factory.

But whether you are short or tall; big or small; have brothers and sisters or you're the only child in the family; whether you are white, black, brown, yellow, or Native American; whether you are religious or not; whether you have a mom and a dad who adopted you or parents who gave birth to you; whether you are raised by one parent or two, or by a grandmother—no matter what kind of family you're in, what counts is that people in your family love you and you love them.

Just because parents of one of your friends got a divorce doesn't mean it will happen to your family, and if your parents are divorced, you shouldn't think that it will happen to you when you become an adult. Even though your parents don't seem to get along and they have decided not to live together, they still love you and they still want to be your mom and dad and take care of you. They just won't do it together.

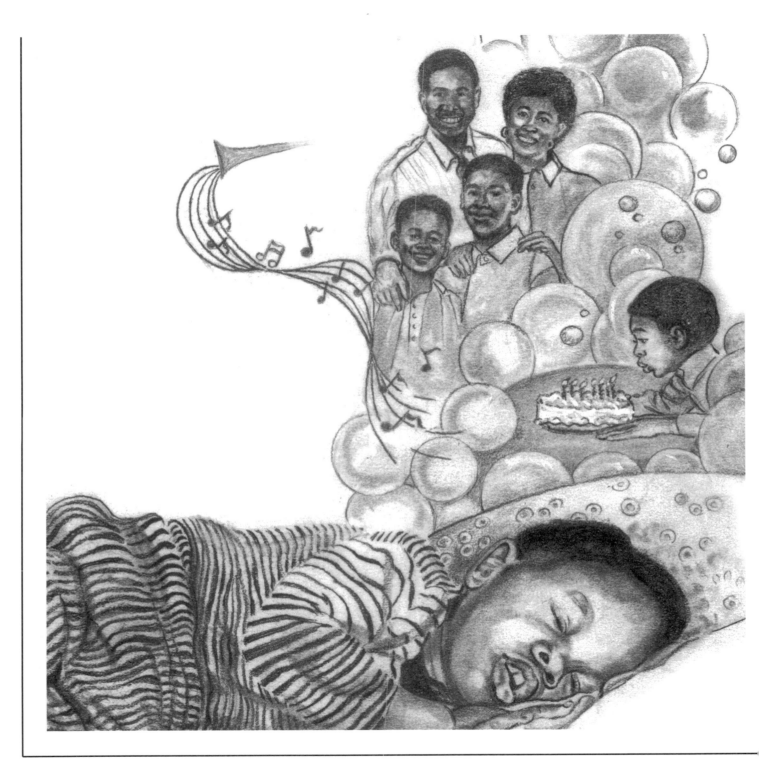

In your dreams you can make up your own special family—the one you might have one day when you grow up.

Don't forget to imagine how you and your family will face problems. Solving problems is part of life and a great way for moms and dads and brothers and sisters to get to know one another better and to learn what each person is good at.

Your parents or teachers have told you at some time that you don't need to be like anyone else to be happy. You just have to be yourself. This is also true of families. Your family doesn't need to be like someone else's family to be filled with love and hope and kindness and laughter. It just has to be the right family for you!

And if your family has changed because of divorce or illness or any one of the many other things that happen to families as the years go by, just remember that it isn't easy for any family member to get used to changes. But talk to each other. Let your family know how you feel. When they know how you feel, then they can help you and you can help them to handle the changes.

It isn't always easy to live with a new parent or parents. It may take time before you feel good being with each other, and you may need to talk many times to explain to each other how you feel about many things.

Everyone has to work together to make a happy home. You too! No matter what kind of family you're in, what is really important is whether the people you live with love you and you love them.

No matter how or why you have the family you live in now, you couldn't choose it. So don't feel bad if things aren't what you expect. Again, if one or both of your parents couldn't take care of you—it was not your fault. If one of your parents died or left and didn't come back—it was not your fault. Your job is to live your life the best way you can. You don't need to be just like anyone else to be happy.

Some children think that if they behaved better, their mom or dad wouldn't have died or their parents wouldn't have divorced or separated. This is not true. The death of a parent or the breakup of a family is *never* because the kids did or did not do something.

You know that all families have their problems, even those where children live with both their parents. You may think that someone else's family is better than yours because the moms and dads and kids *seem* to get along so well. But these families aren't better than yours. You just don't know about the problems they have. Maybe your family looks great to your friends, but you know that brothers and sisters, moms and dads don't get along all the time. This doesn't mean your family isn't best for you.

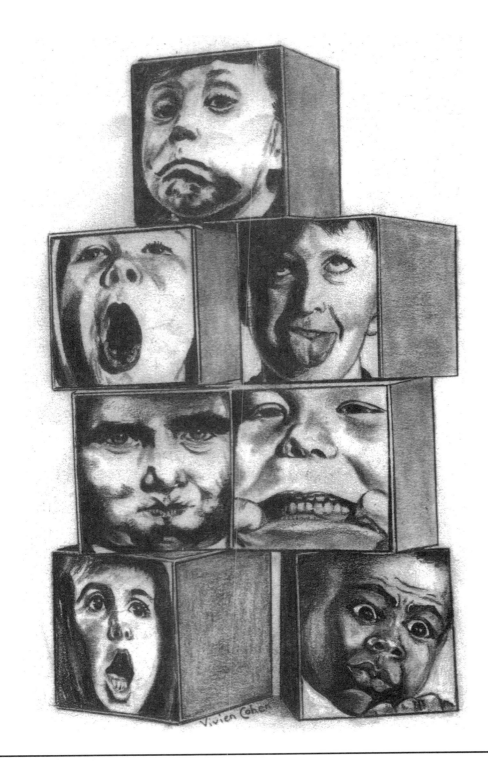

Vivien Cohen

If you don't get along with someone in your family, even if it's not your fault, you could try to make things better by acting nicer, trying to understand their side of things, or helping out. Try it! Everyone likes to be treated with kindness—someone has to start it—it might as well be you.

It's also up to you to be the best person you can be. How you do in school these days, the way you make friends now, and how you explore the things that interest you like art, music, reading, or sports will make you a better adult or parent when you grow up.

If other kids tease you because your family is "different," just say, "Yeah, they are! All families are different. Besides, I like my family just the way it is. We love each other and I wouldn't trade them for anything."

Here are some things you can do if you're not happy now: Try talking about what worries you or makes you sad. It's best if you could talk with your parents, but if not, talk to someone you trust, like a teacher, a friend, or a relative. Try talking about what troubles you by saying how you feel, like "I feel sad because . . ." This works better than getting upset and starting a fight or just staying by yourself and not saying anything at all.

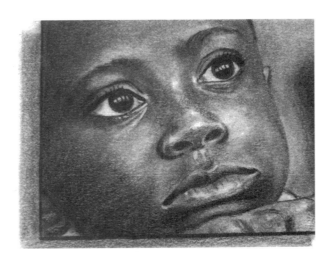

Another good thing to do is to write down what you're thinking about or make drawings about how you feel. Sometimes if you're lonely or sad, it might be a good idea to get a pet like a dog or a cat (you'll have to get your parents' permission first), and of course you have to treat your pet like it is your best friend, with lots of love and care.

Vivien Cohen

Another idea is to take care of the garden, or collect things like stamps, sports cards, or other stuff. Instead of watching TV a lot, learn something new like swimming, making brownies, or surfing the Internet on your computer. You could also join a club like the scouts or be helpful to a handicapped kid in your neighborhood. The main thing is to try to be kind and not to be angry or upset. Keeping busy with interesting things makes everything in your life easier.

If bad things happened to you when you were growing up, *decide right now*: when you have a family of your own, you'll be nice to your children. If you will continue to do the same bad things that were done to you, you will always be unhappy.

If you are doing the right things, you will be full of energy and you will be nice to people. If you are not doing the right things, you'll be tired and bored a lot and you'll be mean even to people you like. So if you want to change your feelings, try being kind to people, and especially to your family. Wonderful things will happen to you.

Vivien Cohen

So what do you think? Is your family normal? Well, you guessed it. THERE IS NO SUCH THING AS A NORMAL FAMILY. Every family is different, and since there are no perfect people, you can be sure that there are NO perfect families.

And besides, differences are what make life interesting!!

See if you can get this last idea:

Don't compare yourself with anyone else. You are a special person with your own right to be happy.

Draw a picture of your family.

Draw a picture of your favorite place to visit with your family.

Draw a picture of your family's favorite holiday.

Draw a picture of your favorite pet or animal.

Draw a picture of your home.

Draw a picture of your school.

Draw a picture of you.

Draw a picture of your friend.

Draw a picture of your favorite hobby or activity.

Draw a picture of your favorite toy.

Draw a picture of the family you want to have when you grow up.